COMFORTABLE SLAVES -WAKE UP! ONCE YOU DO, ITS HARD TO GO BACK.

MANOJ CHENTHAMARAKSHAN

ISBN 979-888521051-5

All of humanity!

Contents

Foreword

Oh yes, Most of us are slaves in this society. Most of us distract ourselves not to look at reality. Few are not even aware that they are slaves. This book has been written with a single intention to help people break the bubble they have around them, to realize their potential, and live life on their terms.

I could have made this book into a 300 pages book with 30 chapters, but I decided to keep it simple and be precise about what is to be conveyed.

Rather than surviving, human beings are supposed to live on this planet earth. We have surpassed the urge to survive long back. At the level of advancement that we live in currently, we are supposed to live beyond what the teachers and scholars have left us.

It all starts with awareness. At first, we need to learn how we are slaves in each area without realizing it. The image has been created such that we are not slaves, but we are, and we deep down know it is true. Rather than confronting it, we tend to escape from it by distraction.

I wouldn't take the complete credit for creating this book, because it was inspired by leaders who have expressed these views in the past. Am just expressing it with my view.

"Everything that needs to be said has already been said. But since no one was listening, everything must be said again."

— André Gide

I welcome you to this book with an open mind. :)

Acknowledgements

Special thanks to Sneha Murali, who inspired and supported me to write this book

CHAPTER ONE

EDUCATION SYSTEM

"We are students of words: we are shut up in schools, and colleges, and recitation -rooms, for ten or fifteen years, and come out at last with a bag of wind, a memory of words, and do not know a thing."
— Ralph Waldo Emerson

Sit in a row, wear a uniform, stand in line. You will be punished if you disobey, don't question; instead, follow what I say.

These are said in two places, jail and schools. The education system followed widely is creating employees to work in industries. Whereas the industrial age has surpassed, but the system remains the same.

As soon as I speak this topic to the public, the common say is, *"Ohh, students learn to be disciplined in school."* I know how important it is to be disciplined, but we impose discipline on them before realizing what the child really needs. Rather than allowing the child to explore their dreams, we try to inculcate discipline in a very early stage.

Discipline is essential, but self-realization and self-expression are much more important. Like our fingerprints, every soul is different from one another. There are potential engineers, musicians, artists, architecture, philosophers, etc., in the future generation. Rather than helping them figure out what they wanted to do, we try to discipline them.

"Everybody is a genius. But if you judge a fish by its ability to climb a tree, It will live its whole life believing that it is stupid."
- Albert Einstein

The above quote written by Albert Einstein is practically true even in this modern age. The system is not diverse enough to understand the potential in each individual.

I still have no clue why I learned $(A+B)^2 = A^2 + B^2 + 2Ab$. I haven't applied this in real life till now. But during my childhood, Elders told me that if I didn't know this, I was dumb. For several years I believed it to be true.

Years are passing, and I am still waiting for a day when I will apply this formula in my life. The mathematical formulas created by geniuses are of profound value for people working in that sector.

What does it have to do with an author or a salesperson?

But it is mandatory to learn it! Why? No one knows why because they were taught so. The cycle then passes on to the generations that come by.

There is a secret but forced rule implying that there is just one way and everyone should walk through the same journey.

Origin of education:

During the early ages, cavemen used to hunt regularly to survive. It took years to figure out that some foods could be stored and eaten after a few days. It took time for them to realize hunting daily is not required. Cavemen passed this information down to their children to reduce effort.

Later they realized the potential of farming where they could plant seeds. Wait for a few months and yield food for months. This was passed down to their children. For their children not to go through the same rough period they went through.

Education was widely spread to have a quality life. From the invention of the wheel to the latest mobile phone, the core aim is to simplify life.

Yet right now, we are more focused on grades. *Where did we lose our way?* Through my research, I understood that *"The law of Conformity"* caused this issue.

The Law of Conformity:

The law of conformity is a herd mentality. When 9 out of

10 people are doing a particular activity, even the other one repeats what the rest does. We try to fit inside the social group constantly.

Human beings are diverse. Humans have the ability to think, and each one of us is different from one another. But the law of conformity has reached the level where following a group of people is normal and standing apart is abnormal.

Right now, it is about fitting into the crowd. Human beings are not supposed to live this way. We have the ability to think and act creatively. Don't get into the assumption that education is just for school students and college students. Life itself is a teacher for us. Learning is a daily process.

"Formal education will make you a living, Self-education will make you a fortune."
-Jim Rohn

So what to do now?

1. Self-realization
2. Expert

Self-realization:

"Your own self-realization is the greatest service you can render the world."
-Ramana Maharishi

It is vitally essential for you to realize who you are deep within. What does your soul want to express to this world? Who are you? What do you like? What do you value?

These questions are to be promoted at an early age. In contrast, most individuals ask these questions after completing school and college. I had to take a long turn. I asked these questions after working for two years. Yet some say I am too early. I have coached people in their mid 50's. I once heard a person say that he was living a life just to please their peers in his entire lifetime.

How sad is it, right? A person living the whole life just to realize that they lived just to fit in? Now, listen! You don't have to wait till your 50's to ask these questions to yourself, Do it right away. *(if you are in 50's never too late, You never know if you will get another chance to visit planet earth with this body. Follow what your heart says NOW)*

For a teacher to preach about self-realization, the teacher/ educator should have gone through self-realization. But usually, it is not the case though. They give less attention to the teachers who craft the future generation and wonder how the society got fu*ked up.

Some parents/teachers say, *"oh, children make mistakes, we need to guide them, we can't let them..."*. Of Course, they make mistakes, but it is from mistakes they learn. Adults resist children from committing mistakes.

Haven't you learned the best lessons by committing mistakes? Let them make some mistakes as well. That is how everyone realizes. Your love for the kids should not stop them from self-exploration. Be a guide but not a commanding officer.

"Speed without knowing the destination would result in chaos."

Promote children, even adults, to self-reflect and self realize who they are. Each of us holds a unique gift within us. It is our responsibility to find it for ourselves. No one else would do it for us, even this book will make you question and wonder, but the answer has to be written by you.

It is tough to write an answer *"Does the Big Bang violate the 1st Law of Thermodynamics? Does uniting computer science with astrophysics make humans immortal?"* compared to *"What do I like?"*

What if I am wrong, and what if my interest changes?

"The one who falls and gets up is stronger than the one who never tried. Do not fear failure but rather fear not trying."
Paulo Coelho

LET YOUR IDEAS EVOLVE. Before you try all the flavours in an ice cream shop, you can't conclude that your favourite is bubblegum mint. Take time to explore some of the flavours. There are flavours such as Belgium chocolate, red velvet, black current, choco mint, vanilla, strawberry, etc... Some might be good to smell but not that great when you eat. Some might be good, but others can be better. **Just explore**

And once you find your favourite flavour, it's bliss, right? For the next 15 minutes, you will not look at what others are eating. You will be in your own la la land.

After a few days, your friend will take you to a better ice cream shop, and your views may change. You may find choco mint even tastier *(well, that's my favourite, if we meet at some point, you now know what to get me)*. Ok, so stop thinking about ice creams and compare them with your life now.

When time passes, our perspective changes, our vision towards life changes. It's pretty normal. But don't consider that as a "dabbler."

Before I chose to become an author, I have tried Photography, Graphic designing, Video editing, 3D modelling, Fashion technology, Reiki healing, Tai chi, etc. I had to explore myself in all these realms to understand where I could blend my passion and purpose.

We have the liberty to explore ourselves with the help of the internet. All you have to do is decide the field you need to study. You can do it right away by searching for the courses on google. Seriously, it's just a few taps away.

Check out my latest book, "Know Thyself" it is all about exploring yourself and finding the authentic "YOU." It contains 99 powerful questions which could unlock your real potential. *(and yes, I am promoting my book. Thank me later)*

Expert:

"Whatever you are, Be a good one."
-Abraham Lincon

Once you choose to pursue a particular field after realization, you should step into the realm of expertizing in it. Become the best version in the domain that you have chosen.

Best compared to whom and what?

Best compared to who you were yesterday.

I happened to research experts in different fields. I was trying to find the common string attached with all of them. It was "Curiosity"

Remember when you were a kid you were so curious to play a video game. Even when the opponent smashed you a million times, you never gave up. You were so curious to find a loophole to surpass the level? Well, you had a profound quality during your childhood.

It is curiosity that makes a person excel in a particular field. Being a kid again gives you the ability to get up a million times yet stay curious.

(Note: Now, don't try to impose this information on your kids or your friends. Please do it for yourself. Your transformation is the best inspiration for them.)

"Be the change you want to see in this world."
- Mahatma Gandhi

CHAPTER TWO

WORK

"Your work is going to fill a large part of your life, and the only way to be truly satisfied is to do what you believe is great work. And the only way to do great work is to love what you do."

- Steve Jobs

People work for a job they don't like, please people they have no respect and are too scared to get kicked out of the job they hate.

Who are comfortable slaves here? The one who knows that they are stuck in life, who doesn't like how things are working out in the workspace yet still hides their emotions and acts as if everything is going well.

And, there are a set of people out there who are waiting for the weekends to come. Why weekends? Because they say that weekend is when they feel alive. So, what it means is that five days in a week they are so dead. The majority of the crowd end up drinking to numb their minds from the pain caused. And the hypocrisy is that it is called "Reality" or "Normal life." According to whom?

"The worst thing about slavery is that the slaves eventually get to like it."
- Aristotle

And there are these other people who don't drink but do other activities such as hiking and riding. It is true that you get energised when you do them. But they don't realize that they are just escaping their reality for 2 days but stuck for 5 days.

You are not designed to live a life like this. Just because your friends and peers live, the same life doesn't mean that you will have to live the same.

Why do we call them comfortable slaves?

Because they are 'comfortable' being 'slaves,' sometimes they forget that they are stuck inside a jail where they drill you and make you do what they think you should do, Tirelessly for hours in the day.

We are not talking about a passionate person who loves their job and progressing forward in their dreams. We are talking about individuals who are bored to death, feel they don't fit under a cubicle and feel they are wasting their lives working in a job they won't be proud to tell their grandchildren.

"I freed a thousand slaves. I could have freed a thousand more if only they knew they were slaves."

- Harriet Tubman

Remember that you can always be replaced

Did you know that you can always be replaced by someone new? There are millions of people standing in the same queue as you have stood once. Corporates have a ton of people who could do the same job as you do. If the time is right, they won't think twice to let you go.

"The weak are meat, and the strong do eat."
- David Mitchell, Cloud atlas

This is a powerful quote that shook me to realize the so-called strong controlling a majority of the weak's. Although it may seem normal in the modern world to have a corporate lifestyle, when you look deep into their eyes, you see slaves hidden with a smile on their faces. (I am sure you know someone with whom you could relate this with, share this book with them.)

There are tons of companies that have done this to maintain the equilibrium of the company. They can't pay a hefty salary to everyone. There is a person waiting for you to quit so that they can do the same job for half your salary.

Don't make them realize!

"I didn't know I was a slave until I found out I couldn't do the things wanted."
- Fredrick Douglass

Slavery has ancient roots in history and still exists today in many different forms. Slavery was never abolished, It has only evolved into a new form.

Some companies have this basic rule that they will never let you realize that you are a slave. They have an HR team to make you feel comfortable, to empathize with you, by taking you on vacation, have team dinners, and have a fancy retreat once in a while. They do this not just for you to feel comfortable but also in a mindset to spend more money to fit into the surroundings (fancy places). (I do have HR friends who are genuine and don't exploit, I am referring to only evil corporations with a fake smile to please you. If you are a Genuine HR, you wouldn't get angry at these statements, would you?)

Just to fit into this social circle employees start to overspend, use credit cards, buy cars, get loans that are not necessary. They had to bear the unresourceful expenditure. And guess what? To pay the bills, they continue working for a job they hate doing.

This forms a vicious loop, and people get stuck in it. Just to escape this rat race for a short period, Some start the habit of drinking, and since they have a habit of overspending, they tend to get stuck in an ever-ending loop of slavery with a fake smile.

Don't fight for a job that you hate

I was this person who hated what I did, Still persisted in sticking around and ensuring that I wouldn't be kicked out. Whenever I had a meeting with my superior, I had these thoughts at the back of my mind, "What wrong did I do this time?" "I think they are about to kick me out" "Oh god, how will I pay my debts if I am kicked out."

A few months later, I realized that I was fighting hard not to get chucked out of a job that I really hate doing. If you are this person who is trying so hard to stick in for no reason.

Here is a message for you. What is it all about? Why are you doing this? Life is too short to fight for something that you don't like. Stop self-sabotaging.

It's for the money:

I do understand. I am indeed living in the same society where money plays a vital role, which I don't deny. If I had denied it, I wouldn't have sold you this book. I should have given it for free. But I didn't do that. I am of course, charging for the book.

What I am trying to convey here is to follow your passion and start generating money through it. If you research people who live their life by doing what they love, you will start to see a whole new world. There are millions of people who are pursuing their passion and are earning loads of money.

Yes, of course, you can earn money by following your passion, meaning what you love to do.

Is it going to be easy?
No, Maybe yes!
But is it going to be worth it?

Hell, yeah!

Is it too late now? Can't think about escaping at this stage of commitments? Start slow. Spend 1 hour a day on your passion project. Don't have 1 hour? Wake up 1 hour earlier by not binge-watching your favourite series/ scrolling social media endlessly during late nights.

How will the world operate if everyone starts to follow their passion?

"Pleasure in the job puts perfection in the work."
-Aristotle

This is my favourite topic. Not everyone wants to quit their 9-5 job. Some people really love their work. I had the same question in my mind. If everyone started doing what they are passionate about, then who would do the monotonous work? Who will do works which are tiring and stressful?

The world is so diverse; not a single person's interest matches exactly with another person. There are people interested in engineering, mathematics, physics, business, carpenter, gardening, mechanic, etc,. Ask the next 10 people you meet where their interests lie when it comes to work, you will be surprised by the variety.

So, do people like to work for someone? Doesn't everyone want to build their own business? Or Be on their own? This questioning was pondering over my mind. And then I came across "Intrepreneurs"

Intrepreneurs:

The term "Intrepreneurs" was coined very recently. Intrepreneurs are people with an entrepreneurial mindset who work under an organization. They are people who challenge the status quo and work to make their customers and team members lead a better life.

I met a girl once who was working in an accounts department. We were discussing corporate culture. She gave me a different perspective on corporate. She told me about her job and how she loved solving problems in her workspace every day. I was astounded by the answer when she said she loved her job. She even quoted, "Work is a game for me."

I had a roommate back when I was working for a company. He had this really cool car with a huge paycheck, and to my surprise, he was genuinely happy. I had a chance to discuss it with him over some drinks. I asked him, "How are you happy working in a corporate?". He said that he is looking forward to going to the office each day.

He was so passionate about cloud computing. He later showed me a collection of tutorials that he watched for months to educate himself on cloud computing. He was not educating himself out of pressure, but there was a genuine interest in his work.

I then realized everyone has a role to play, and some individuals also like even corporate culture. They were working for themselves even when they were working for someone else.

What if you are not an intreprenuer?

That's ok. Everyone is unique in this world, and each one of us has different things to dedicate to the world. Bring out the magic in you.

In the early days, we had a barter system where people exchanged products for survival. If you were good at fishing and I was good at climbing trees. I would give you some coconuts for the exchange for some fish.

I do understand that we can't exchange coconuts in Starbucks. But what if I tell you that you can earn money using your skill?

> What if you can find what you love?
> What does the world need?
> What are you good at?
> And what can you be paid for?

(I would strongly recommend you to find your IKIGAI. Do read the book or research on this topic. Ps, I don't get any commission for promoting the book).

It is not that only the legends such as Einstein, Steve Jobs, Jeff Bezos, Mark Zuckerberg, Will Smith, and Oprah kind of people have a unique skills within them. They are people who have found their passion, protected it, and nurtured it.

Still, have doubts about what I say? Do your own research on successful people in Fiverr and Upwork. You start to see a whole different world.

There is no one single path to be successful. It's a myth. Wake up!

"Honour your calling. Everybody Has One. Trust your heart and success will come to you."
- Oprah Winfrey

CHAPTER THREE

RITUALS AND RELIGION

Why do we pray to God? Who is God? Why should we thank God for the food before eating? Why is it necessary to encircle the shrine?

These were some of the deep questions which were running in my head since childhood. We all would have had these questions at some point in our childhood. I dared to ask my family members and teachers. No one was able to give me a concrete reason. Instead, everyone started imposing on me that It must be following these rules without questioning. I found it really hard to do that.

A few years later, I concluded that God doesn't exist because no one was able to give a concrete answer about him/her/it. Others seem to be ok to follow God without knowing the reason behind it. I begged to differ.

Later in the years, I stumbled upon the Law of attraction, which gave me a comprehensive picture of this invisible power controlling our lives. I happened to research this topic endlessly. The dots slowly started to connect. I was introduced to Neville Goddard, where his interpretation of the bible gave new perspectives about how I saw the whole of religion.

I started connecting the dots and realized the power of words, The power of intention, and habit. I respect all religions now; although I haven't researched them all, I have gained respect towards them.

It's true that some religions are backed up with science. You will be surprised when you find the reason behind certain practices. I am not saying all the practices do have scientific reasons. Some are superstitious and purely under false belief.

I don't want to explain the science behind the practices in this book. But I realized that religion originated for a good reason. It taught humanity about kindness and how to live harmoniously.

I personally see gods as teachers who have taught us some of their profound knowledge. As time passed, we started glorifying the teachers but ignored the knowledge. There are other cases where the knowledge has been so glorified that a strict rule of practices is imposed without teaching the reason behind it.

I really like buddha's teaching. Although many see him as a religious leader, I have viewed him as a wise atheist.

He even told his followers not to blindly follow whatever he said but instead question logically and find the answers until they were satisfied. Self-analysis was taught during the Gauthama Buddha's period. Even Buddhism has been misguided and practised in different forms in different places currently. As information is passed on to another, there is a deletion and distortion which occurs and is inevitable.

People in this modern age should bring this habit of questioning. **Don't question to oppose but question to understand.** It is a common trend to question nowadays just to oppose and spread hatred. Don't fall under the category of hatred, Fall under the category of hunger to understand.

Who are the comfortable slaves here?

I am referring to slaves who follow certain systems without understanding the reason behind them. Question and understand the reasoning behind each activity. If you don't like to follow, well don't.

This hunger to understand may lead you to different religions, or you may find your home in your own religion, or you may create a new religion. Whatever gets you to live a content life.

But, never ever ever have this ideology **"My religion is the only way."**

No, it is not the only way. Like how nature is diverse, every individual has their own path. The maturity to accept others for who they are would enlighten you.

The problem arises when one set of people start preaching their God is mightier than others. **There are preachers in the name of unity, breaking humanity.** Become mature enough to identify these dangerous preachers.

In the end, we are all living in the same world. The food that you are consuming is brought to your plate by different people with different religions. Love all of humanity and protect your kindness irrespective of what religion is opposed.

Some leaders try to diversify this in society's minds for personal gain. **Please beware of the ones who claim they protect Peace as they kill others.**

My view about God:

He is my close buddy *(Yes, I quoted "him" because it's my imagination).* I get in touch with him quite often. Sometimes I lose him when I get confused, When I get anxious, when I am not in my natural state, I lose the connectivity.

But then I realized he was not out of reach, but I was polluted by the mind, which made me think he was far away.

When I take a deep breath and become aware of the present moment, I start feeling him. Yes, I see the God within me, residing in me.

His silence made me think he was absent, but it took years

to understand that he was teaching me his language to communicate with him.

"The Kingdom of God is within you."
-Leo Tolstoy

Not in a group of men or some elites or the one who does religious practice for 12 hours in a day. But within everyone. I don't think I have to be of a particular gender or race to witness God in me.

I do visit religious places, I also do some religious practices as well. I view God as a teacher who once taught us how to become conscious.

My perspective of viewing God may be different from yours. I will not ask you to follow my religion, nor should you. Let's respect each other's choices and live life harmoniously for our future children to come. Let them not be polluted by the dogma created as such to protect religion. (I don't want to discuss this topic as I want to live in this world for a lot of years, Peace :P)

CHAPTER FOUR

CONSUMERISM

"Advertising tries to stimulate our sensuous desires, converting luxuries into necessities, but it only intensifies man's inner misery. The business world is bent on creating hunger which its wares never satisfy, and thus it adds to the frustrations and broken minds of our times."
~ Fulton J. Sheen

We think that we would be happy when our needs are met. But it is a never-ending loop where the number of products increases at our house, but the mind tends to seek more like a monkey trying to chase the stars.

Dopamine, Smartphone and you:

There is this trio of love encircling our society nowadays. Have you seen people who endlessly scroll? Have you seen people constantly tied up to their phones by either sharing content or consuming them? Are you one among them?

These social media apps are built for both kinds of people. The ones who create and the one's consume it.

The one's who create content:

Let's talk about the one who creates it, when a person clicks a picture and posts it in their feed. Their mind seeks social validation in the form of likes, shares, comments, saves, etc. This pattern of social validation gives a sense of purpose for a person in society.

Just to get noted and validated, some people go the extra mile to criticize themselves. For what? Just to get recognized and acknowledged. Why do you think people do this?

There is this dopamine release when an individual does this activity.

Dopamine is a chemical produced by our brains that plays a vital role in motivating behaviour. It gets released when you eat your favourite food, when you have sex, after you exercise, and most importantly, after you have a successful social interaction.

When you post on social media, when you get validation from society, this dopamine instantly gets released, making you feel good. When this is repeated, it forms into a behaviour where you start to believe your happiness lies when you get acknowledged. Trust me, these companies are well aware of your psychology; they seduce you by making you believe you are a red carpet celebrity.

What about the one who consumes it?

An information and opinion overload is happening for the consumers who randomly consume data. Your brain can only make a limited number of decisions in a day. After which, you become restless and tired.

Researches say we make 226 decisions each day on food alone. It is estimated that the average adult makes about 35,000 remotely Conscious decisions each day.

New studies are being done, which suggests we take more than 35,000 decisions. Well, you don't need to know the precise number as a common man. All that you will have to understand is that you make a lot of decisions in your waking life, which shape your future in return.

Remember Newton's law? For every reaction, there is an equal and opposite reaction? **For every decision you make, you give birth to a new future.** So, It's time to take responsibility for your decisions.

So next time when you use the Internet, make sure you "Use it" rather than "It using you!".

That's the reason people like Mark Zuckerberg wear the same outfit every day. They simply avoid making unwanted decisions because they know the value of making decisions. *(What an irony, right? if you know what I mean)*

Magicians use this technique of making your brain do 5-7 tasks in a short period, which makes your brain go into a snooze mode. As soon as this happens, they command you to sleep. And this giant body falls on top of the magician- like a chopped meat. This happens due to decision overload. That's the reason why you feel tired after a few minutes of scrolling.

"The reason you're stressed is because you don't keep your awareness on one thing at a time."
-Danadapani

The social media apps also are designed to predict what you would like. It uses algorithms to show you different contents at different times during the day. Remember that the AI is learning about you. More than your friends or family, your phone knows all your secrets.

Why do they collect it? There are many reasons for these, but importantly to sell your habit to industries. In a layman term, when you are this person who loves to travel, and if the AI identifies your pattern. It shows you ad's related to travel. Traveling accessories, hotel discounts, flight discounts, etc.

These apps make the consumers release dopamine regularly to form a habit of visiting their apps frequently to sell you things that you may potentially need or make you believe you need them.

Check your friend's phone. What appears in their feed would be completely different from yours. Imagine billions of people who are using their phones. Each one of their phones has a different pattern of information.

In earlier times, there was one TV, with a regular set of programs to the whole world. The entertainment world has become more sophisticated that each of us gets a personalized show. All the credit goes to AI and the team working behind the AI to make this possible.

Imagine it as feeding an virtual animal with tons of food, and this animal will outgrow human beings one day and make better decisions than humans. It could be a threat or life-saving. The future will teach us the lesson *(Hey, If you are interested in this topic, I would strongly recommend you to watch the black mirror series, and No, I don't get a commission for this)*

Short term pleasure:

No, that burger won't solve the problem.
No, that haircut won't solve the problem.
No, that vacation won't solve the problem.
No, scrolling won't solve the problem.

It has become a trend to shop to reduce depression. People believe that if they buy a particular product, their life will change. But in reality, their surroundings change when they buy things, but the person who uses the product remains the same. Cleaning your mirror won't make you look beautiful!

Most of us are addicted to short-term pleasures. Eating that burger won't solve the problem in your life, but your brain tricks you into believing that that is what you wanted. The brain tricks you into doing so because that is how we have conditioned our minds.

By over usage of social media, we have induced dopamine release in our brain in the short term repetitively. Our brain started believing that short-term pleasures are all there is.

This in return, causes the extension of addiction to porn, alcohol, smoking, and other so-called *"problem solvers."*

"The successful warrior is the average man, with laser-like focus."
- Bruce lee

Escapism:

"An addiction to distraction is the end of your creative production."
- Robin S.Sharma

Most individuals are so used to the pattern of distraction. When they witness a problem in life, they distract themselves rather than facing it. I personally have noticed the pattern in me when I get stressed. I start to swipe on social media for no reason. For years I didn't realize the motive behind this pattern. It took years for me to understand that I was avoiding my problems rather than solving them.

I later realized that I was doing no justice to my vision and goals. But still, it was so addictive that it was hard to stop myself from entering social media.

These companies have behavioural psychologists who

ensure the user stays in their app for a prolonged period of time. Personally, I had to delete the apps to get rid of the habit.

The initial few days were tough, but later I realized the time I had in my life. I needed a digital detox so badly to discover my voice. Currently, I am using social media, of course, but consciously. It's ok to watch funny cat videos once in a while but never make it a habit.

"I call myself a Peaceful Warrior... because the battles we fight are on the inside"
-Socrates

The desire to be happy has been misdirected to short-term pleasure. If you notice this pattern in your life, consciously stop it. The first step is always awareness. Before using the Internet, have a clear intention. Get what you want and step out of it.

"The Internet is so powerful that when a disciplined mind meets the internet, wonders happen."

You lose your authentic self:

"If you are not paying for a product, you are the product"
- Andrew Lewis

When you feed your mind with unwanted information, you start to lose your authentic self; you try to fit in the group and never express yourself.

Everything becomes crafted; you may start to do certain activities based on not what you like but what society implies to be normal.

Before the introduction of the Internet into our lives, our options to think and choose were limited. The Internet helped us to expand our mind's to the infinite possibilities of information.

But the question is, are we ready for this level of exposure? Are we mature enough to choose what we want to consume? That's why too much knowledge is also dangerous.

Imagine your mind like an eating plate, and the knowledge spread all across the world as a buffet. You have many options, of course, but your plate can fit only a few, so what do you naturally do? Select the food which fits under your plate. You can reload it again if you are like me (I love food). But your tummy starts to indicate to you that you have reached a limit. If you try to stuff more, then you know the consequences later that day.

Likewise, Choose what you consume. You may think it is time pass, but remember that your mind is rewiring as you do this so-called "Timepass". You become what you consume.

Perspective overload:

Each one of us views things differently. Not a single person in this whole world sees the same things as a person sees.

We filter the information through our belief system. We simply delete, distort and generalize when we load in information.

Imagine a beggar approaching for money in real life:

Person 1: Oh poor guy, let me offer him some coins

Person 2: Let me buy him some food; I don't want him to misuse the money.

Person 3: He looks fine; he can work. Why should I pay my hard-earned money?

Person 4: I think he is a CBI officer in an undercover operation

Person 5: He could be carrying some disease; I don't want him to touch me

Person 6: This must be a prank show. Where is the cameraman?

Person 7: I am not going to give money or food. Let me call the officials to get him a proper homestay.

Person 8: Why doesn't he sell something? Let me get him 10 pens so that he earns through selling.

Person 9: Huh!

Person 10: Does it even matter? We are all going to die in 2021.

What did you understand by the above examples?

It's all perspectives that are formed based on the belief system. Each belief system was created based on an individual's past experience.

Are you wondering how this is related to the chapter Consumerism? Where in I talk about psychology?

This is happening on the Internet currently. People have started expressing their views; as a matter of fact, the Internet is flooded with millions of content with opinions.

Power of saying yes/ Power of saying No / Power of being silent

Why you should work hard? / Why you should work smart? / Why you should not work at all?

It's all about them! / It's all about you! / there is no You or them

Even this book is about my perspective which you have invested your attention. But you have consciously decided to purchase it, set a time aside, and read it *(if you are reading a pdf version, Buy it, You know it's not expensive, right?)*

It's your attention that is valuable in the realm of the Internet. The more you give your attention, the more they can earn money out of you. I don't want to talk about the monetization of the internet industry; you can google them.

My interest is towards you!

Check this example:

A woman makes a cupcake recipe video, and the comments she has received are as such:

- Aww, beautiful.
- Does it just look good, or does it even taste better
- I don't like the lighting
- Why is the video creator so lame?
- Hit Like if you think this video is lame
- Cute one
- Her smile is so fake
- Who thinks editing is horrible, hit like
- The background music is pathetic; check my youtube for cool music copyright-free.
- Dumb
- They are promoting sugar intake, dislike

Each perspective is different from one another. Some may like it, hate it, disrespect it, criticize or even condemn it. Does everyone have a positive outlook to take only the best and leave the rest?

The statistics don't show that. It's an increasing threat among teens to get depressed and have low self-esteem when discouraged.

Of course, you can show your passion work on the Internet and get a million views through it. But I just wanted to remind you that everyone's perspective is different; ensure you don't get mentally disturbed because of these. In my products and books, I have witnessed the same.

Check my books -

"25 small habits",
"55 questions to ask yourself",
"Know Thyself"

Products -

"Dream Believe Create Planner",
"Positive Planner"
and "Habit tracker."

At Amazon, they have both 1-star ratings and 5-star ratings; I see a major difference in perspectives when I read them. I accept those reviews; if they are constructive, I learn and improve; if it is purely negative, I laugh at it and move on. Just become mature to understand that everyone has their own perspective.

Beware! Cocaine or any other drug is labelled as illegal; social media is not labelled as such as of now. It is a drug too.

Choose what you want to consume!
Pigs eat anything and everything; Lion chooses its prey!

CHAPTER FIVE

THE GRAND ESCAPE

Although we have already spoken about how to escape being a slave in the above chapters. This chapter is to sum them all. The first step is, of course, to be aware.

Self-awareness:

"Your own Self-Realization is the greatest service you can render the world."

- Ramana maharishi

All this information is of no use if you don't relate it to your life. Information stays as information if not reflected upon. Take a moment to reflect on your life.

Ask these questions to yourself in all these areas.

Education, Career, Religion, Consumerism

1. How was I a comfortable slave in the past?
2. What beliefs did I have in the past?
3. What do I realize now?

Take time out to just think. Get in touch with yourself, Talk with yourself and build a good rapport. Start journaling your thoughts. When you start to see results, rather than sharing them with others, share them with yourself, and expand further. **Before you start to express it to the world on how a person should be, become that person!**

Your friends or family members may not realize the importance of it as you do. So don't let others influence you and discourage you. And also, Don't try to rescue others while you are rescuing yourself. It's a good act to save others but not before saving yourself.

Remember this safety dialogue during flights? Where they say to put the mask on yourself at first and later help the person next to you? Yes, you must put on your own oxygen mask before assisting your parent, sibling, partner, or child. Initially, I thought it was crazy selfish!

The truth is, putting your oxygen mask first does not show a lack of love or care for others. Instead, you can help others only when you are secured.

FORGIVE YOURSELF:

> *"Unexpressed emotions will never die. They are buried alive and will come forth later in uglier ways."*

- Sigmund Freud

You will have to forgive yourself for not taking action all this while, for getting alluded to by society, for not being authentic to yourself.

We tend to escape this phase by distraction. Distracting yourself with unresolved emotions would erupt in the future, causing issues for yourself and your surroundings.

"Forgive yourself for the bad decisions, for the times you lacked. Understanding, for the choices that hurt others and yourself. Forgive yourself, for being young and reckless. These experiences are vital lessons. And what matters most right now is your willingness to grow from them."

-Marcandangel

The reason why forgiveness comes before taking action is that the guilt would stop you during the process. Many individuals get motivated by reading a book or listening to a speech and plan to take action. 95% of them end up failing in the first week. This happens due to not forgiving their past self.

Acknowledge that the mistake has happened. Forgive yourself deep down. You may feel the relief in minutes which a counsellor would have to do for ten years. It's free of cost. Just do it.

DISCIPLINE & RITUALS:

Once you get clarity about yourself and what it is that you

wanted. Develop a habit around it. It may be difficult at the beginning because of the instant shift in a routine. Take it slow and back it up with rewards. Bring a habit of reviewing every week. Just to ensure that you are not losing track.

Many individuals fail when it comes to building a habit, they have a huge list of to-do's that they haven't done earlier. Don't be hard on yourself. Start with a small habit; if you fail to execute it for a day, that's ok.

It's ok if you had that fries with your friends, forgive yourself and start the diet from the next day. Just because you failed one day doesn't mean you will be a failure for the rest of your lifetime. I like to put it this way *"Just because you were a** hole one day doesn't mean you have to be for the rest of your life."* **Forgive yourself and bounce back up quickly.**

You may evolve:

During this Journey, you may tend to get new insights about yourself and change your perspective. It is quite natural to undergo this process.

In the initial days of self-exploration, I wanted to be a graphic designer, then it shifted to photography, and later it evolved into a life coach. I had to explore my options to decide which one resonated with me the most. It may not be the same in the future, and that's ok.

Well, you need to understand that evolution is a natural process. You can't be the same person who was a year back. Life is teaching us, and we are evolving daily.

Ensure that you are evolving and not dabbling; you can identify this by looking into your past.

Choose what you consume mentally:

Not just calories, also start to count your screen time.

"The word consumer says it all. The one who consumes is known as the consumer. So, when you are using your phones, you are consuming as well. That's why you are called a consumer"

What happens when you consume 10,000 calories per day? How would your body look after a year? Well, compare it with your overconsumption of data. Imagine what your mind would look like. I could only imagine a big fat baby asking for more food.

Choose what you want to consume. If you need to educate yourself on how to grow and water plants, Go to the website/app, type it, choose the content, consume it, and leave it. Come to the real physical world and practice it.

Don't watch the recommended videos. The AI is trying to predict what you might like based on what you have typed. Don't encourage it. Just leave when you got what you need.

Trying to compete with 1000's of engineers with behavioural psychologists is a tough battle.

Check your screen time once a week to check your consumption level. If you feel like overconsuming, put a screen limit on the app. If you think the apps are seducing beyond the app limit. Just delete it.

Get off the grid if needed and if it fits your future lifestyle!

Hire a coach:

"A life coach does for the rest of your life what a personal trainer does for your health and fitness."
- Elaine Macdonald

To sum it all up and bring to a final conclusion, most of your hurdles can be avoided by hiring a life coach.

Hiring a coach is the best decision that you could ever make. Being a coach, I have a coach for myself for whom I am accountable. Now don't confuse yourself with a coach, counsellor, and mentor. Each one of them plays a different role.

There are different names a coach has for themselves nowadays like Transformational coach, peak performance coach, Money coach, Health coach, Holistic coach, this coach and that coach.

A life coach is a general term. Coaching is a process through which you will understand more about yourself and about your visions in life. Unlike counselling, where they focus on your past, Coaching concentrates mainly on the present and the future.

Coaching is not about advising or giving solutions; a coach would rather help you come up with your own solution. The coach simply asks you questions and facilitates you during the Journey.

The majority of the Athletes, Peak performers, Entrepreneurs, and celebrities have a life coach. A good coach finds the strength in you and creates a personalized plan just for you. Often we can't handle it all by ourselves. If we have a person to whom we are accountable, we tend to do better work. Just hire one.

Beware: Just be cautious while hiring a coach, Have some background check in advance. Some counsellors claim to be a coach. Ensure you get the right one. Don't look for cheap ones; look for the best ones.

Find yourself and be yourself.

Have a purpose in life and stay flexible in reaching the destination.

Express your true self, The whole world awaits to witness you.

You never know if you will get another ticket to visit planet earth, so live here, Live consciously, Live now!

Conclusion

Hope you enjoyed the book while reading because I loved when I wrote it.

If you care to support me. Please do leave a review. It helps others to decide whether to purchase or not. It also helps me to understand your perspective and would encourage me to write more books.

So do leave your honest review. Criticism is welcomed. Love to see 5 stars and 1 star nearby. It's all perspectives right? I welcome it.

Let's stay connected, You can also follow me on Instagram "**manoj_the_coach**"

Subscribe to my youtube channel "**The Moral Science Teacher**"

Buy my other books on amazon:

25 small habits,
55 Questions to ask yourself and
Know thyself

Also you can check my store **www.thepositivestore.co**

And have a great day after leaving a review :P

9 798885 210515

Printed by Libri Plureos GmbH in Hamburg,
Germany